ALL ABOARD AMERICA

Monticello

A Buddy Book
by
Sarah Tieck

ABDO
Publishing Company

VISIT US AT
www.abdopublishing.com

Published by ABDO Publishing Company, 8000 West 78th Street, Edina, Minnesota 55439.

Copyright © 2008 by Abdo Consulting Group, Inc. International copyrights reserved in all countries. No part of this book may be reproduced in any form without written permission from the publisher. Buddy Books™ is a trademark and logo of ABDO Publishing Company.

Printed in the United States.

Contributing Editor: Michael P. Goecke
Graphic Design: Deborah Coldiron
Cover Photograph: Photodisc
Interior Photographs/Illustrations: iStockphoto.com (pages 5, 7, 11, 20, 21); Monticello.org (page 9, 12, 15, 17, 19, 22); Photodisc (pages 13)

Library of Congress Cataloging-in-Publication Data

Tieck, Sarah, 1976-
        Monticello / Sarah Tieck.
            p. cm. — (All aboard America)
        Includes bibliographical references and index.
        ISBN 978-1-59928-937-3
        1. Monticello (Va.)—Juvenile literature. 2. Jefferson, Thomas, 1743-1826—Homes and haunts—Virginia—Juvenile literature. I. Title.

        E332.74.T54 2008
        975.5'482—dc22

                                                        2007027268

Table of Contents

CHAPTER 1

A Historic Home

Monticello is a famous **plantation** in Virginia. It was the home of Thomas Jefferson. He was a very important American.

Jefferson was a **patriot**. He lived during the time when the United States was becoming an independent country. He is famous for writing the **Declaration of Independence**. And, he served as president of the United States.

West Entrance

East Entrance

Thomas Jefferson designed Monticello. He lived there with his family from 1770 until his death in 1826.

Jefferson called Monticello his "**essay** in **architecture**." The house was full of his ideas. Even now, it reveals much about the famous man who built it.

Building A Dream

The name *Monticello* is an Italian word meaning "little mountain." It refers to the **plantation**'s location on a hill near Jefferson's childhood home.

The land was a gift from Jefferson's father. For many years, Jefferson dreamed of building a house on his family land. **Architecture** was one of his many talents.

In 1767, Jefferson started **designing** his house. In 1770, workers began Monticello's first building. This small, brown cottage was called the South Pavilion. Inside was a small, single room.

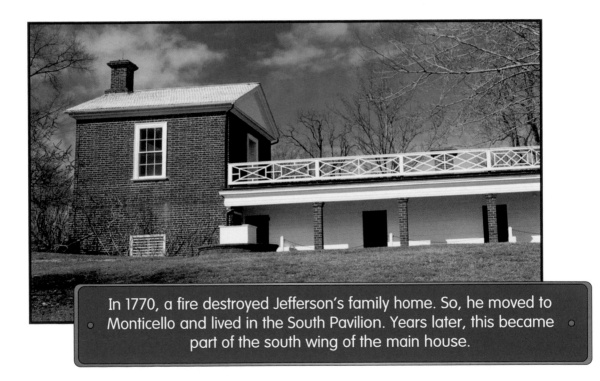

In 1770, a fire destroyed Jefferson's family home. So, he moved to Monticello and lived in the South Pavilion. Years later, this became part of the south wing of the main house.

For 40 years, Jefferson lived in the White House and other places. Still, he spent much of his time improving Monticello.

Jefferson **redesigned** parts of the main house. He also added the North Terrace. And, he expanded the South Pavilion.

In 1809, Jefferson finished his term as president. So he moved back to Monticello. He continued designing and changing Monticello until his death in 1826.

Hundreds of people helped build Monticello. Some were free workers and others were slaves. Six days a week, they worked from morning until night.

For many years, Monticello was a **plantation**. Workers cared for animals and created products, such as cloth.

There were also vineyards, orchards, and fields. Monticello's crops included apricots, strawberries, pecans, rice, and corn.

Jefferson was interested in science and learning. He did **experiments** on some of his crops. These tests helped him improve farming and design a new, faster plow.

More than 330 kinds of vegetables and 170 types of fruits grew in Monticello's gardens. These gardens provided food for the people who lived and worked at Monticello.

Inside Monticello

Monticello's main house was very large. It had three levels and 33 rooms. Eleven rooms were on the main floor. These included the dining room, the tea room, and the parlor.

Jefferson's bedroom and study were right next to each other on the first floor. Jefferson slept in a little area between the two. He called this his cabinet.

In 1805, Jefferson installed a piece of circular glass in the dome. It was four feet (1 m) wide. Because of this, the room beneath the dome was known as the "sky-room."

When people think of Monticello, they often think of its dome. Jefferson got the idea for it from French **architecture** he had seen. He built Monticello's dome in 1800.

Learning was important to Thomas Jefferson. So, he used his house to educate people about the world.

When visitors arrived, they came into the entrance hall. Here, Jefferson displayed Native American items and natural **artifacts**, like in a museum.

Because of his love of learning, Jefferson owned a very large library. There were more than 7,000 books in his book room!

Many of the items in the entrance hall were from the Lewis and Clark expedition. Jefferson planned this exploration of northwestern United States.

During the **War of 1812**, many U.S. government books were destroyed. Jefferson sold Congress his library for $25,000. This was the start of the modern Library of Congress.

CHAPTER 5

Ideas And Inventions

At Monticello, Thomas Jefferson's ideas came to life. Many of these ideas made life easier for people. Others connected people with important information. Some are still used today.

Jefferson's calendar clock displayed the day of the week. And, his turning bookstand could hold open five books!

Jefferson's famous dumbwaiter was tucked into a cabinet on the side of a fireplace. It was often used by the servants.

The dumbwaiter is a small mechanical elevator. It carried supplies from the cellar to the dining room. Dumbwaiters are still used today to help people save time and work.

Daily Life

Life at Monticello was very busy. Jefferson got up at sunrise. After eating breakfast, he worked in the gardens or wrote letters.

Monticello was a working **plantation**. So, there were many chores to do. Jefferson managed money, records, and workers.

In addition, Jefferson took notes about the weather, his crops, and his **experiments**. He also built new inventions for Monticello.

Parts of the north wing provided storage for many of the supplies needed for daily life at Monticello. Soap, candles, wine, and olive oil were stored in the cellar. Carriages and ice were also kept there.

Detour ⬇

Did You Know?

. . . Thomas Jefferson is pictured on one side of a U.S. nickel, and Monticello is on the other side!

. . . Thomas Jefferson died at Monticello on July 4, 1826. It is still possible to see his tall, gray gravestone in Monticello's cemetery.

. . . After Jefferson died, his family had to sell Monticello to pay many debts. Uriah P. Levy bought the house in 1834. The Levy family took care of Monticello until the 1920s. They are said to be the first people to protect and preserve a historical place!

Today, the main house and the grounds of Monticello are a museum. They are filled with objects from Jefferson's life there.

In many ways, the story of Monticello is also the story of Thomas Jefferson. Visitors can learn about this great American and his life's work of creating Monticello.

Today, more than half of the furniture at Monticello once belonged to the Jefferson family. There are also many new pieces of furniture designed to resemble Jefferson's original pieces.

architecture the art and science of planning and designing buildings.

artifact an object made or used by people that has historical value.

debt money owed to someone.

Declaration of Independence a very important paper in American history. It explains that America is ready to rule itself as an independent country.

design making a plan to create something.

essay writing that explores an idea in depth.

experiment a test carried out to discover something new or unknown.

patriot a person who has a great love for his or her country.

plantation a large farm.

War of 1812 a war between the United States and the United Kingdom from 1812 to 1815.

WEB SITES

To learn more about Monticello, visit ABDO Publishing Company on the World Wide Web. Web sites about Monticello are featured on our Book Links page. These links are routinely monitored and updated to provide the most current information available.
www.abdopublishing.com

Index